What's Wrong With Her?

**A Black Man's Guide To Understanding, Evaluating, &
Healing The Black Woman Vol: 1**

By Aaron Fields

ISBN: 978-1-953962-18-8

CONTENTS

<u>Something To Think About Before You Read</u>

In order to reach fulfillment in life, the black man must evaluate himself, nourish himself, and invest in himself first. Once you understand the nature of the black woman, you won't have time to go back and forth with her. You won't have time to hate her; you won't have time to resent her. Above all, you won't have the time to worship her or develop an unhealthy obsession.

----------Aaron Fields

Word From The Author

Before you continue reading, let me start off by informing the readers and the audience that this book is not about black men versus black women. The intention of this book is to give you valuable insight and information that can help you cultivate a healthier outlook. If you are here looking to create confusion, anarchy or even start a gender war, this is not the place for you. Sadly, there are too many public platforms and forums that create toxic interactions between black men and women.

People who promote chaos on these platforms usually have a deep-seated resentment towards the opposite gender. Therefore, they are incapable of loving anyone. Their behavior stems from their desire for attention and their inability to overcome personal struggles. When it comes to dealing with black women, the onus is on us as black men to look at ourselves in the mirror and learn how to think and operate on a higher level. Why? Many of us black men display toxic traits. Our emotions are out of balance, we are angry, confused, hopeless, and spiritually broken. Too many black men are walking around feeling self defeated and choosing to partake in self-destructive behavior. Sadly, many of of us are embracing toxic ideas that are destroying our women and children in the community.

A lot of black men appear to be confused when it comes to the behaviors and thought processes of women (particularly black women). It's important that black men as a collective get out of their comfort zone and start thinking on an optimal level. Once you elevate your way of thinking, your mindset will prevent you from being destroyed and traumatized, especially by women.

In life, when you put too much unnecessary time and energy into something or someone, it can stop you from ascending to a higher level of wisdom. Wisdom is something you're going to need in order to have a rulership mentality. If you continue to get perplexed by the machinations of women, you'll never have stability in your life.

Instead of using all of your time and energy obsessing over women, use your time to augment your mind, body, and spirit. There is nothing wrong with wanting to become healthy and stable in every aspect of your life. Once you become the best version of yourself, you won't have that many issues with women.

It might not be something you guys want to hear, but part of our role as black men is to elevate black women, but not in a way that's kowtowing, or forced. To put it another way, when the black man has achieved balance and stability in his life, the black woman will be elevated. Once the black man gets his life in order, the black woman is likely to be more receptive and willing to listen to the black man. Unfortunately, our actions have caused black women to become emotionally detached, which explains why they no longer trust us.

Too many black men worry too much about the things that are beyond their control. A lot of black men don't understand the difference between reality and delusion, especially when it comes to women. While it's important to love and care for black women, we also have to understand that they don't belong to us. What do I mean by that? What I mean is that nothing in this world is permanent. One minute, the woman loves you, and the next minute she wants to kill you. From a spiritual perspective, it may be beneficial for you to pray to God for the capacity to accept and comprehend the swift changes of this world.

It's important for black men to understand that the black woman is not a Goddess and she's not God. It's important to note that black women are beautiful and can bring tremendous value to the world. Unfortunately, many of them are broken, unstable, and follow certain ideologies that are pervasive to the black community. The black man must take on the responsibility of thinking and operating at a higher level, to assist both himself and the black woman. Now, if you're one of those black guys that have no interest in helping or healing black women, then this book is not for you. The black man must ensure his own life is stable before attempting to help the black woman heal. The black man must strive hard to achieve good health and stability in all areas of life (such as mental, emotional, physical, financial, and spiritual).

Is there any kind of racism embedded in the structures of this society? Yes, to a certain degree. However, in order to overcome the system, the black man must foster an optimistic atmosphere in his home. He must be a confident leader, and he must create ways to help others in his community instead of harming them. If he has a spiritual side, he must enhance his relationship with God. Now think about this for a second. If each black man puts together a set of standards and ethics that will benefit the black community, we will be overwhelmingly powerful. If we want to succeed, we must be ready to humble ourselves and take responsibility for our actions.

It's not meant to be disheartening, but some of us in the black community will not make it. Sadly, as it pertains to black women, many of them are depressed and angry. Many of them are so broken and unstable that attempting to assist them can become detrimental to your own life. If you're a black man that is well respected in your community and aspiring to do great things, it might be in your best interest to avoid these types of women. Always remember that in life, you can't save everyone. Sometimes, helping others can backfire and cause harm to yourself. I know this sounds harsh, but in order for you to reach any level of success in this world, you must embrace solitude. Am I saying you should never be in a relationship with a woman (black woman)? No, I am not, because whatever you decide to do as a man is your business. However, I believe that it's important to be selective about the type of woman you want to be intimate with, especially if you plan on having kids with her. In the meantime, focus on yourself, manifest your gifts, and think about what you want to do with your life.

.

No matter how frustrating black women might be to you, always keep them in prayer and be patient with them. Maybe one day the most high God will change their hearts because most of them are angry, lost, depressed and mentally unstable. It's important for black men to understand that black women are living in complete darkness and they need healing. If we want to get them out of that darkness, then we, as black men, must make sure we don't intentionally bring any form of instability and negativity into their lives. Your job as a man is to solve the problem, not create it.

Seek Wisdom First

If you are a man of wisdom, consider it to be a blessing. Having wisdom means you have a great understanding of the world around you. In order to be at the pinnacle of understanding, one must not only seek worldly intelligence, but spiritual intelligence.

If you are wise, you will come to realize that you understand the black woman more than she understands herself. Most black women don't want to hear this, but as a black man, it's your obligated duty to know the black woman more than she knows herself. Why? It's not enough to just love and heal the black woman. You must be able to correct her when she is wrong and understand her emotionally.

It is important for black men to understand that black women are not obligated to heal us, and this is understandable. Why? Many black women are already battling psychological and spiritual issues in their individual lives. The issue with black men is that many of them don't rely on a spiritual entity for enlightenment and understanding. Instead, they make the mistake by depending on the black woman to speak life into them and solve all their problems. It's essential for the black man to look to God and heal himself first, and then assist the black woman in her own healing.

Black Women Don't Respect Black Men

Do the vast majority of black women no longer respect black men? Do the vast majority of black women reject black male authority and black male leadership? Yes, they do because you see it on social media, television, in the workplace, and in the household. Keep in mind when most black women claim to be "pro black" or "woke"; it's all just an act. If black women truly value black men, they would exhibit it more towards the ones who reciprocate the feeling. On the other hand, due to many black men developing self-destructive tendencies, feelings of inadequacy, low self-esteem and self-hatred, it makes since why most black women don't respect us. Black men, as a collective, must start seeking a higher purpose in life in order to gain respect not only from other people, but from themselves.

In order for the black man to gain his respect from black women, he must learn how to love himself and develop discipline. Black men must know when to walk away and say no to certain things (sex, drugs, violence, toxic relationships, etc.). Unfortunately, most black men struggle with discipline and refuse to reject things that are not good for them.

The black man must understand that if there's anything in this world that might sabotage or destroy him, he must get rid of it. You must continue to focus on developing yourself financially, physically, mentally, emotionally, and spiritually. It's important that you brothers understand that there are going to be certain women you must watch out for. When a low-quality woman sees that you are achieving great things and you're trying to better yourself, she's going to bring chaos into your life. Please understand that a real woman is going to fit into your life by making things better for you. If you are dealing with women that are not concerned with your well-being and happiness, then you need to get rid of them and move on with your life.

Life is already challenging and stressful, so it wouldn't make sense for you to bring someone toxic into it. Please understand that many of these women out here love confusion and destruction. Therefore, the black man must establish order and the rules of engagement with the women he deals with. How do you do it? By sticking to your standards and core values from the very beginning. If they don't respect your standards and your core values, all you need to do is leave the relationship.

You Don't Have To Argue With Her

One of the major things that some black women hate and have trouble dealing with is constructive criticism. If you try to criticize or hold some black women accountable, they may react by accusing you of hating black women or creating a gender war. Now, when it comes to black men, we must acknowledge the fact that many of us are not receptive to constructive criticism as well. In fact, many of us refuse to seek help or self-reflect. Black men must understand the importance of looking out for one another and holding each other accountable. Black men should remember to give black women feedback that is helpful and not demeaning. Above all else, if you give a black woman advice, make sure you don't contradict yourself or come across as a hypocrite. Perhaps if more black men took the time to humble themselves, maybe black women will follow suit.

If a black woman's attitude towards you turns negative, there are two things you can do. First, you should never go out of your way to disrespect or harm her intentionally. Remember to always think and not be too impulsive. Why? Well, because it's not worth it and you don't want to make a decision that you'll regret later on. Second, you should never entertain the idea of going back and forth with a woman in a heated exchange. Why? It's because some black women (or women in general) love arguing with black men. Remember, the nature of the woman is that she's capricious, chaotic, and unpredictable. This explains why a lot of women are so infatuated with negative energy and arguing. Constantly going back and forth with women is an indicator that you're not being productive in your life. In addition to that, always going to war with women makes you look bad as a man overall because it shows that you have no self-control.

As a black man, there is no shame in walking away or refusing to argue with women. Getting into a meaningless argument or altercation with a woman is a manifestation of the man's weakness. If you're going to engage with women, make sure it's with someone you truly care for (like your Mom, sister, or significant other) or else it's a waste of time. Hell, even if it is with a woman that you care about, you really shouldn't be arguing with her that much in the first place. Now, are you going to argue a little and disagree with the women that come into your life sometimes? Yes, but getting into fights and insulting one another is completely unnecessary.

The Fall of Man

For those of you guys that are biblical, you'll know that in the book of genesis (Adam & Eve), Satan came into the garden to trick and manipulate Eve, not Adam. Why? Well, from a biblical standpoint, in order to destroy the man, you must corrupt the woman. Keep in mind that even though Eve sinned first, God questioned Adam. Why? Well, because Adam was the leader and responsible for Eve.

As a man, you can't put the woman on a pedestal like Adam did in the bible. If you do, you'll try to appease and pacify women every time, which is not healthy. That's why Satan focused on tricking the woman, because Satan knew Adam revered Eve. If a man worships a woman, he'll do anything she wants, even if it's detrimental to his health and well-being.

This biblical concept also applies to the black man. Think about it, a major reason the black community is in disarray right now is because black men have an unhealthy obsession with black women. In other words, instead of black men augmenting themselves and focusing on their growth, they decide to invest too much of their own energy into women.

In the black community, the woman is ahead of God and the man, which is not correct. From a biblical standpoint, the chain of command is God, Christ, man, woman, child. Why? Well, it's because when the man is in his right state of mind, and he's spiritually mature, he's going to know how to keep things peaceful and in order. As a man, your job is to love, honor, respect, and cherish your woman, not become overly infatuated with her.

Are Most Black Women Spiritual?

Do most black women really believe in God? If so, why do some of them seem spiritless? If you don't understand who you are as a person and you don't understand the laws, commandments, and standards of God, your prayers have no meaning (**read proverbs 28:7**). It's fair to say that in a spiritually malnourished society, spirituality has now taken a backseat to other priorities. As a result, there is chaos, confusion, and a lost connection.

Yes, the black woman should be treated with love and respect. However, always keep in mind that she is not your God. Believe it or not, some black women think they are Gods, that's why they love to worship themselves. Sadly, many of you guys love worshipping women as well, which makes you part of the problem. The black man must understand that he should never allow his idolatry of a woman to distract him from achieving great things in this world.

Gentlemen, please understand that some women are chaotic. Because a lot of women are broken and mentally ill, many of them become easily susceptible to anything. Although women are beautiful human beings, many of them love to promote anarchy.

One of the biggest reason a lot of black women lack spirituality is because of how black men treat them. Our self-destructive tendencies and degenerate behaviors have caused our black women to be spiritless. As a consequence, many black women have become emotionally disconnected from us. Another reason many black women are not spiritual is because many black men are not spiritual. Without faith and a strong spiritual identity, life can be a lot more troubling and confusing. It is important to encourage the spiritual development of black men. Why? Well, because it has the potential to positively affect their relationships with themselves and black women. A major perk to being spiritually healthy is that it can help you deal with tough situations more appropriately. Black men who have a spiritually healthy attitude towards black women can provide them with a sense of peace, purpose, love, and forgiveness.

When you're with a black woman, your job is to love, honor, respect, and cherish her. It's not fruitful to be a source of instability or negativity in a black woman's life. If the black woman you're with is good to you, you should be ready to love and care for her.

Your job as a man is to protect your woman, even if it means you have to protect the woman from herself. Most black women will not admit this, but they are counting on us as black men. Yes, there are plenty of black women who are smart, successful, and can take care of themselves. However, I'm sure if you ask most black women, they would want to be with a good man that symbolizes peace, order, and wisdom rather than being alone. If the black woman can't count on you, the relationship is over. That's why it's important for the black man to not start a serious relationship with a woman if his life is not in order yet. A black man should not enter into a serious relationship until he is physically, emotionally, mentally, financially, and spiritually stable. Getting into a serious relationship with a woman when you're not ready only perpetuates the stereotype that black men are not real men.

ADVICE FOR THE BLACK MAN

Most women, especially black women, are angry, lonely, and depressed. Some black women can't maintain a healthy relationship with black men because they spend too much of their time trying to argue and confront black men. Make sure you guys never allow yourself to get caught up in a toxic relationship paradigm with these women. Why? Well, because black men should never be in a relationship with a woman who is constantly bringing him stress. Gentlemen, if you're constantly getting angry, upset, and stressed with the woman you're with, do yourself a favor and leave the relationship, because it's only going to get worse. Look for ways to make your life more tranquil and peaceful. Sadly, many of you guys have taken so many years off of your life because y'all were taught to embrace toxic relationships. If the woman you're currently dealing with doesn't respect you as a man, leave the relationship, pray for her, and wish her the best of luck.

Feel free to share your thoughts right here: _____

_____

_____

_____

_____

_____

_____

SOMETHING FOR THE BLACK MAN TO THINK ABOUT

If you're a black man with a strong spiritual connection, there are many ways to help invigorate black women who are lacking spiritual energy. One of the first things you can do to help black women connect with their spirit is to teach them how to love themselves. Encourage black women to not think low of themselves and help them understand that having a negative mindset can lead to a diminished spirit. You also want them to believe in their full potential and let them know that they have a lot to offer to the world. Be aware that she could become emotional on this journey. If she does, that's okay. Allow her to let her emotions come out. If she has something to share with you that touches her heart, let her share and encourage her to not hold back her tears, especially if they need to come out.

What are your thoughts?

_____

_____

_____

_____

_____

_____

_____

_____

Don't Be A Weak Minded Black Man

A major reason most weak minded black men partake in self-destructive behavior is because they know it attracts certain women. That's why I mentioned in the previous chapter (chapter 4) that if you put the woman on a pedestal, it will lead to your demise. Gentlemen, I cannot stress this enough; your mind must be focused on higher things, preferably spiritual things. Why? Well, because that's the only thing in this world that will remain consistent in your life.

If you're a black man that is astute, upstanding, authentic and pretty much on point with everything in your life, you will appear rather strange to some women. As a black man, if you come across a woman that is always disrespecting you, then stop interacting with her. Keep in mind there are plenty of black women that will love you for being your true authentic self. Women reciprocate respect; if you don't show it, you won't get it.

In some cases, when certain women run into a man that has his life in order, they'll view themselves as unworthy and will eventually find some way to sabotage the relationship. That's why when they get older, they regret their past decisions and realize they should have stayed with the man that actually treated them well. Unfortunately, this is the story for some of these women. Men should be conscious of the cycle that often occurs in relationships regarding makeup and breakups. When you opt to get back with the woman after the breakup, it is important to not dwell on the issues that were present in the previous relationship, particularly if you've already decided to get back together with her. If you're going to keep bringing up the past, then maybe it's time for you to end the relationship and move on.

Don't Get Random Women Pregnant

Now, if you're dealing with a woman that you're not serious about, don't make the mistake of planting your seed into her. I say this because it's important for you guys to understand the situations you're in before they happen. You don't want to end up having unplanned children with a woman you've never held in high regard.

The world doesn't need more children being raised in unhealthy environments with two parents that don't seem to respect one another. These are the situations that can easily be avoided when the man empowers himself by thinking and conducting himself on a much higher level. As a black man, you must think with your head and not your penis. The last thing you want to deal with as a man is a toxic and stressful relationship with a woman that you didn't see a future with.

Please understand that as a black man, the onus is on you to make the right decision. If you are going to get a woman pregnant, you must know who she is and why you're getting her pregnant. The repercussions of getting the wrong woman pregnant can affect your offspring for many years to come. As a result, you'll create a dysfunctional community. Is this the type of community you want to create for yourself? Is this the type of legacy you want to have? Please understand that having a child when you're not ready can affect your life in a traumatic way. The reason black men are at the bottom of the totem pole in society is because black men are not breaking the cycles appropriately. If you don't have any children right now, it's no rush. Take your time before deciding to impregnate a woman; don't rush it, especially if you lack the resources or are not ready to provide optimal care for a child.

Are Black Women Strong?

Are black women strong? Yes, they can be. Once black women understand the true essence of their strength, they become more valuable. However, in order for black women to be strong, they have to be in their right state of mind.

The black woman has a rare and distinctive beauty that makes her one of a kind. The issue with the vast majority of black women is that they can't embrace their true femininity. Why is that? It's because there are too many weak minded black men. It's the black man's job to bring peace, order, leadership, and structure into the community. Black men have to change themselves if they want black women to change.

Sadly, the black community is in disarray right now. Why? Due to our self-destructive tendencies and failure to love and communicate, black men and women are taught to compete, argue, and fight with each other. As a result, the little respect black men had for themselves is now gone. Therefore, black women, along with the rest of society, see no value in us. Black men must stop complaining and concentrate on ways to succeed in society, instead of arguing and competing with black women.

Do Most Black Men Act Like Women?

A major problem in the black community is that most black men act like women. Why? It's because a lot of black men grew up in fatherless homes. The vast majority of black men grew up around a lot of estrogen. Because of the lack of a strong male role models, a lot of these boys are exuding feminine traits and are getting influenced by a lot of low level thinking men.

Black men have often been taught to think and act like women, so they lack the skill of being assertive. Unfortunately, a lot of black men lack the ability to think logically and analyze facts. Hell, most black men will get emotional and try to argue or even start a physical altercation. Therefore, the black man looks very weak and pathetic, as opposed to being a logical thinker and a powerful leader.

I understand that many of you black men grew up in rough environments, and many of you are experiencing tough times right now. Because of the trauma that most of you guys have been through, some of you are probably angry at women. Maybe you guys are angry at yourselves or your fathers. Hell, maybe you guys are angry at God. Whatever situation you brothers are going through, please understand that I want all of you guys to prosper. I hope and pray that all of you can see the bigger picture and don't self-destruct. Please understand the importance of black men having a positive presence in the household, in the community, and even in society.

As long as black men continue to act and think like women, they'll never be able to lead their black women. Why? Well, it's because a black man acting like a black woman will only lead to emotional arguments and unresolved issues. That's why it's important for black men to

not go back and forth with women. I promise you, it's nothing but a distraction.

Where Do Some Black Women Get Their Influence From?

There are many shows, music videos and movies that are crafted specifically to appeal to black women. Guys, if you watch these films and television shows closely, you'll see that they depict the black woman as someone delusional. Why is that? It's because they're breaking the fourth wall. Society is well aware that television has a great influence on women. Many of these films, music videos, and shows are meant to push women to behave immorally and promiscuously. As a consequence, many of these women are dealing with the effects of severing strong ties with good men. The reason for many failed relationships among women is due to not only the shortage of quality men but also their dependence on the misinformation and disinformation given to them.

Black women's female friends and relatives, who struggle with maintaining healthy relationships, also influence them. It's an unusual occurrence for women to be held accountable for the broken relationships they were part of. Sometimes, when things get "mundane" and "dull", they get prompted to leave the relationship. The reason many women are receiving horrible advice from other women is because misery loves company. In other words, some women don't want to see other women happy. That's why it's important for the black man to take charge, lead his community, and preside over his household appropriately. That way, he can be a good example for his daughter by demonstrating what a good man is supposed to look like and how to maintain a healthy relationship.

Knowing Your History & Culture

Do you know who you are? Do you know where you're from? One of the most important things to have in this world is knowledge and information about your culture and your history. With the exception of Black people, particularly African Americans, most cultures in our society have the privilege of creating their own historical narrative.

In order to have a powerful culture, you cannot let other demographics create your history. When you have a different race of people creating a different narrative about you, that means they have power and control over you. As a black man, do not let anyone else dictate how you should live and what you should believe in.

Due to low self-esteem and confidence, black men and women seek guidance and answers from other demographics. A major reason these other groups of people have control over us is because we're easily receptive to everything they say. Sadly, the vast majority of black men and women actually care what other demographics think about them. Why? Well, I hate to admit it, but it's because most black people are seeking validation from them. Yet we, as black people, are still wondering why we're not getting any respect from society. As it pertains to black men, please understand that seeking validation and approval from other people does not get you any respect; it only makes you look weak and pathetic.

The Black Man Must Know His Role

Although there is some level of systemic racism taking place in this society against black men, most of our issues stem from the horrible choices we make. That's why it's important for us to focus on the things we can control and change on our own. Black men's disinterest in restoring order in the community perpetuates the ongoing cycle of chaos in the black community.

Even though many black women are chaotic, destructive, and mentally unstable, ultimately it's not all their fault. You know why? It's because there is no one present to restore order. Therefore, the onus is on black men. The reason the onus is on the black man is because it's his job to be a leader so he can correct and heal the black woman. When the man comprehends the essence of the woman, he will no longer be furious, resentful, or hostile towards her. Why? Well, because he will be knowledgeable about how she functions. This will make him more preoccupied with accomplishing his own ambitions.

Once again, because of the spiritual and psychological battles black women go through, the onus falls on black men's shoulders to be more stable. Unfortunately, most black men can't do it because many of them are destructive and confused as well. When a black man grows up in a single mother, matriarchal, or toxic environment, it becomes difficult for him to correct the black woman because he exudes feminine traits just like the woman. Most black men that grow up in this matriarchal system are struggling to figure out the correct way of living. Deep down, most black men are searching for that patriarchal mindset. As a black man, there is nothing wrong with having a healthy patriarchal mindset, as long as you're a loving person, not breaking any laws or harming anyone.

From a biblical standpoint, in order for Satan to destroy peace, order, and structure, he must exterminate the man by corrupting the woman. In order to destroy the black community, the black man has to be weak and spiritually broken. In order for the black man to maintain his sanity, he has to keep God close to his to heart; and he has to stop seeking validation from others. The black man also has to stop waiting for this society and other demographics to change their ways. The only thing that the black man can change in this world is himself.

Notes

END